Bugs In the Backyard
By: Malique Douglas

Copyright © 2023 by: Malique Douglas
Publisher: Poitier Wordsmith Academy…
Poitier Publishing Company
All rights reserved. No part of this book may be reproduced or transmitted in any form or by any means, electronic or mechanical, including photocopying, recording, or by any information storage and retrieval system, without permission in writing from the author or publisher.

ISBN: 9798399153575
Printed in the United States of America.

Neo and Jayla went into the backyard to play when they saw a ladybug on a leaf.

Neo ran to get the magnifying glass off the outside table to get a closer look at the ladybug.

Neo was in awe, as he noticed the red and black color pattern on the ladybug. Neo and Jayla took turns looking at the ladybug in the magnifying glass then the ladybug flew away.

Jayla said let us look for more bugs in the backyard. Neo and Jayla searched the backyard and came across a fat caterpillar.

They went up to the caterpillar with their magnifying glass and Jayla said wow. I like the green on this caterpillar.

Neo and Jayla kept on searching for more bugs in the backyard. They kept searching until they made it to where the laundry room was and what they saw made them happy.

A big cocoon with a beautiful butterfly with a red and white pattern. Jayla was shocked at how bright the colors were.

Jayla thought she would get a closer look at the butterfly.

So, Neo gave her the magnifying glass and when she got close, the butterfly flew away.

Jayla was sad but Neo just said let us keep looking, there may be more bugs around the yard. She smiled, got up, and they kept looking.

When Neo and Jayla searched the yards some more, they came across a branch and on this branch was a centipede. Neo said "wow, look at all the little legs," but Jayla on the other hand was disgusted by it.

Neo laughed and tried to pick up the centipede but dropped it and let out a scream. All those little legs on the centipede felt like little pricks in his hand, so he dropped it.

Jayla picked it up and put it back on the tree and they continued their search.

At that moment Jayla looked up and saw a golden-brown beehive.

It looked like it had been there for forever, but they never paid attention to it. Then next thing you see a bee start crawling out the hive and flew over to a flower where Neo and Jayla were.

Neo got close-up with the magnifying glass and noticed the bee had little hairs on its body and told Jayla the bee's nickname was furry, she smiled, and they continued their search.

Neo and Jayla went to the side of their house and came across an ant pile and Neo got close with the magnifying glass and touched the pile.

Jayla screamed NO!! And Neo laughed and said their black ants they tickle.

Jayla told Neo he was lucky they were not red ants because they would have bitten him instead of tickled him. The sun was going down after a long day of looking for bugs.

Neo and Jayla decided to go inside, so they went back inside the house.

Their bug adventure came to an end, but you can draw your favorite bug right here...

My favorite bug...

The End....